Y0-EDN-794

Growing Readers

New Hanover County Public Library

Purchased with
New Hanover County Smart Start Funds

SandCastle 2

Opposites

Light and Dark

Kelly Doudna

ABDO
Publishing Company

Published by SandCastle™, an imprint of ABDO Publishing Company, 4940 Viking Drive, Edina, Minnesota 55435.

Printed in the United States.

Photo credits: Corbis, Corel, Digital Stock, PhotoDisc.

Library of Congress Cataloging-in-Publication Data

Doudna, Kelly, 1963-
    Light and dark / Kelly Doudna.
      p. cm. -- (Opposites)
    Summary: Simple rhymes point out the difference between light and dark.
    ISBN 1-57765-145-6 (alk. paper) -- ISBN 1-57765-282-7 (set)
     1. English language--Synonyms and antonyms--Juvenile literature. 2. Readers
(Primary) [1. Readers. 2. English language--Synonyms and antonyms.] I. Title.

PE1591 .D+
428.1--dc21

                                               99-046492

The SandCastle concept, content, and reading method have been reviewed and approved by a national advisory board including literacy specialists, librarians, elementary school teachers, early childhood education professionals, and parents.

Let Us Know

After reading the book, SandCastle would like you to tell us your stories about reading. What is your favorite page? Was there something hard that you needed help with? Share the ups and downs of learning to read. We want to hear from you! To get posted on the Abdo Publishing Company Web site, send us email at:

sandcastle@abdopub.com

About SandCastle™
Nonfiction books for the beginning reader

- Basic concepts of phonics are incorporated with integrated language methods of reading instruction. Most words are short, and phrases, letter sounds, and word sounds are repeated.

- Readability is determined by the number of words in each sentence, the number of characters in each word, and word lists based on curriculum frameworks.

- Full-color photography reinforces word meanings and concepts.

- "Words I Can Read" list at the end of each book teaches basic elements of grammar, helps the reader recognize the words in the text, and builds vocabulary.

- Reading levels are indicated by the number of flags on the castle.

Look for more SandCastle books in these three reading levels:

Level 1 (one flag)	**Level 2** (two flags)	**Level 3** (three flags)

Grades Pre-K to K 5 or fewer words per page	**Grades K to 1** 5 to 10 words per page	**Grades 1 to 2** 10 to 15 words per page

Our shirts are **light**.

We dress the same.

Our shirts are **dark**.

We want to win the game.

My hair is **light**.

I play in the park.

I read at school.

My hair is **dark**.

Polar bears are **light**.

They are hard to see.

A black bear is **dark**.

It climbs a tree.

I have a shadow.

It is **dark** as night.

We play on the beach.

The sun is **light**.

What do you see that is **light** or **dark**?

Words I Can Read

Nouns

A noun is a person, place, or thing

beach (BEECH) p. 19
black bear (BLAK BAIR) p. 15
game (GAME) p. 7
hair (HAIR) pp. 9, 11
night (NITE) p. 17
park (PARK) p. 9
school (SKOOL) p. 11
shadow (SHAD-oh) p. 17
sun (SUHN) p. 19
tree (TREE) p. 15

Plural Nouns

A plural noun is more than one
person, place, or thing

polar bears (POH-lur BAIRZ) p. 13
shirts (SHURTSS) pp. 5, 7

Verbs

A verb is an action or being word

are (AR) pp. 5, 7, 13
climbs (KLYMZ) p. 15
do (DOO) p. 21
dress (DRESS) p. 5
have (HAV) p. 17
is (IZ) pp. 9, 11, 15, 17, 19, 21
play (PLAY) pp. 9, 19
read (REED) p. 11
see (SEE) pp. 13, 21
want (WONT) p. 7
win (WIN) p. 7

Adjectives

An adjective describes something

dark (DARK) pp. 7, 11, 15, 17, 21
hard (HARD) p. 13
light (LITE) pp. 5, 9, 13, 19, 21
my (MYE) pp. 9, 11
our (AR) pp. 5, 7
same (SAME) p. 5

Picture Words

beach

shadow

bear

shirts

Word Families

Words that have the same vowel
and ending letters

-ame	-ee
game	see
same	tree

-ark	-ight
dark	light
park	night

24